What Will Dad

by Cassandra Marcus   illustrated by Jenny Law

◀Harcourt
SCHOOL PUBLISHERS

ISBN 10 0-15-364060-X
ISBN 13 978-0-15-364060-5

4 5 6 7 8 9 10   179   17 16 15 14 13 12 11 10 09 08

Ordering Options
ISBN 10 0-15-364161-4
ISBN 13 978-0-15-364161-9

What will Dad see?

Is it a big bad pig?

It is not a pig, Dad.

4

Is it a big tan fox?

5

It is not a fox, Dad.

Is it a sad cat?

It is me, Dad!

School-Home Connection Have your child read the book to you. Then discuss the games you play with your family.

What Will Dad See?
Word Count: 41

High-Frequency Words	Decodable Words*	
me	a	it
see	bad	not
what	big	pig
	cat	sad
	Dad	tan
	fox	**will**
	is	

Boldface words indicate sound-spelling introduced in this story.